GW00470300

# Antipasti &
# Starter Snacks

ACADEMIA
BARILLA

WHITE STAR PUBLISHERS

# ACADEMIA BARILLA
## AMBASSADOR OF ITALIAN GASTRONOMY
## THROUGHOUT THE WORLD

Academia Barilla is a global movement toward the protection, developmen
and promotion of authentic regional Italian culture and cuisine.
With the concept of Food as Culture at our core, Academia Barilla offers
a 360° view of Italy. Our comprehensive approach includes:

- a state-of-the-art culinary center in Parma, Italy;
- gourmet travel programs and hands-on cooking classes;
- the world's largest Italian gastronomic library and historic menu collection
- a portfolio of premium artisan food products;
- global culinary certification programs;
- custom corporate services and training;
- team building activities;
- and a vast assortment of Italian cookbooks.

Thank you and we look forward to welcoming you in Italy soon!

# CONTENTS

EDITED BY
ACADEMIA BARILLA

PHOTOGRAPHS
ALBERTO ROSSI

RECIPES BY
CHEF MARIO GRAZIA
CHEF LUCA ZANGA

TEXT BY
MARIAGRAZIA VILLA

ACADEMIA BARILLA EDITORIAL COORDINATION
CHATO MORANDI
ILARIA ROSSI
REBECCA PICKRELL

GRAPHIC DESIGN
PAOLA PIACCO

FIRST OF ALL, I'LL SERVE YOU LETTUCE, TO WHET YOUR APPETITE [...] THEN SLICES OF SALTED TUNA [...] ALONG WITH SOME EGGS ON RUE LEAVES [...] AND THIS WILL DO FOR AN APPETIZER.

MARTIAL, *EPIGRAM* XI, 52

# ANTIPASTI

The appetizer, or antipasto, officially begins the dance, whetting the appetite without satiating it. Providing a hint of the courses to come, it is the calling card for the entire menu. The aperitif (a term derived from the Latin *aperire*, meaning "to open") serves to "prepare" the body for the meal.

The custom of the appetizer and aperitif dates back to ancient Rome—*mulsum*, made from wine and honey, was sipped with the dishes introducing the main meal. During the Middle Ages, starters consisted of easily digestible fruits (such as apples), and candies filled with spices such as ginger or seeds of anise, fennel, or cumin, and glazed with sugar or honey. All were accompanied by sweet wine with milk. Yet the concept of the appetizer as we know it wasn't born until the mid-19th century, within the construct of the Italian-style meal. So-called *service à la française* echoed the gargantuan Renaissance and Baroque banquets, in that all the dishes were available simultaneously for diners to sample. Later came "buffet services" (of cold foods), which alternated with "kitchen services" (hot foods). This style was

# AND STARTER SNACKS

followed by the more logical and elegant "Russian-style service" (essentially the same style that is used today), in which the various dishes are served at the table one after the other, in a specific order. And to provide diners a glimpse of what food to expect, and thus to determine the size of their various portions, the menu was introduced.

The appetizer defined as "Italian-style" is traditionally offered as a plate of cold meats (every region in Italy has its own excellent versions), served with vegetables marinated in oil or vinegar, and sometimes offered with butter and fresh fruit (such as the salty-sweet contrast of Parma ham with melon). In this first chapter of the meal, however, the gastronomic genius of Italy is given free rein. Starters can be cold (such as a beef tartare, typical of Piedmont cuisine) or hot (such as a fried torte with roast shoulder of pork, a classic of the Parma lowlands, an area of dense mists and ancient flavors). They can be simple, made from a single main ingredient—a few flakes of Parmigiano-Reggiano, for instance, embellished with a drizzle of balsamic vinegar from Modena. Or they may combine numerous preparations, like the flavorful fried eggs in carpione marinade served with a potato salad.

Even savory pies and focaccias, presented in small pieces—from the *erbazzone* (spinach pie), two thin sheets of pastry stuffed with Swiss chard and spinach leaves, as prepared in Reggio Emilia, to the hearty *torta pasqualina* (Easter pie of spinach, ricotta, and eggs), traditional in Ligurian cuisine—can be excellent for stimulating the appetite, especially when lunch or dinner has an informal tone, without several courses.

Nowadays, in response to changing nutritional needs and the new rhythms of life, the Italian meal is more streamlined. The starter is offered less and less, except at major banquets or receptions. Yet it remains the course served during the rite of the aperitif, a fashion well established in Italy for many years (in fact, a widespread custom since the 19th century, in the bars of Turin, Genoa, Milan, Florence, Venice, Rome, and Naples). It's no surprise that the appetizer—in the form of small, numerous, and varied savory snacks accompanied by a good glass of wine or

ermouth, or by a nonalcoholic drink such as fruit juice—has revealed itself as the true star of these gatherings. Even when the tiny delicacies are not the prelude to a dinner, they satisfy completely as an accompaniment to that most Italian of pleasures, sharing time with friends.

Academia Barilla, an international center dedicated to the promotion of Italian cuisine, has selected 40 traditional recipes or appetizers from the *Bel Paese* ("beautiful county," as the Italians call their home). Some are typical, such as Messina-style fried pizza, Caprese salad, or *gatò di patate* (potato cake). Others are creative variations on classic themes, such as *arancini di riso con scamorza e crosta di nocciole* (rice fritters with smoked cheese and a hazelnut crust), and still others show a delicious novelty, like the bread twists with sun-dried tomatoes and oregano. Some are paragons of lightness, like the salad of spelt with shrimp, while others are heartier, such as the soufflé with Castelmagno cheese. Yet each and every one of them makes an extraordinary prelude to an excellent meal.

# ARANCINI (RICE FRITTERS)

*Preparation time: 30 minutes   Cooking time: 20 minutes   Difficulty: easy*

## 4 SERVINGS

1 1/3 cups (250 g)  **rice**
3 1/2 oz. (100 g)  **smoked scamorza** or smoked mozzarella cheese
3/4 cup plus 1 tbsp. (100 g)  **flour**
1 3/4 cups plus 1 tbsp. (200 g)  **breadcrumbs**
3 1/2 oz. (100 g)  **crushed hazelnuts**, or about 1 cup
3 large  **eggs**
2 tbsp. (30 g)  **unsalted butter**
1/3 cup plus 1 tbsp. (40 g)  **Parmigiano-Reggiano cheese**, grated
3 cups (3/4 l)  **beef broth**
**Olive oil** for frying, as needed

In a large saucepan, boil the broth, add the rice and simmer until the rice is
cooked al dente, about 15 minutes. Drain the rice in a fine-mesh sieve and
transfer to a large bowl.

Stir in 1 egg, the butter and grated Parmigiano and let the rice mixture cool.
Dice scamorza into small pieces. Form rice mixture into balls (about the size of
Ping Pong ball), placing a piece of scamorza in the center of each one.

Place flour in a bowl. In another bowl, stir together breadcrumbs and hazelnuts.
Lightly beat the remaining 2 eggs. Coat the rice balls in flour, then dip them in
the beaten egg and coat them in the breadcrumb mixture.

Heat 1 1/2 inches of oil in a 4-quart heavy pot over moderately high heat until it
registers 365°F on thermometer, then lower fritters into oil and fry in batches,
stirring occasionally, until golden, about 3 minutes per batch. Remove fritters with
a slotted spoon. Place on paper towels to absorb the excess oil before serving.

# GARLIC AND ANCHOVY DIP

*Preparation time: 30 minutes    Cooking time: 20 minutes    Difficulty: medium*

## 4 SERVINGS

*7 oz. (200 g)*  **garlic**, *about 20 cloves, peeled*
*12 1/3 oz. (350 g)*  **salt-packed anchovies**
*1 cup plus 2 1/2 tbsp. (275 ml)*  **extra-virgin olive oil**
*14 oz. (400 g)*  **potatoes**
*14 oz. (400 g)*  **peppers**, *seeded and cut into strips*
*8 3/4 oz. (250 g)*  **cardoons**, *trimmed and cut into strips (optional)*
*8 3/4 oz. (250 g)*  **carrots**, *peeled and cut into sticks*
*8 3/4 oz. (250 g)*  **celery stalks**, *cut in half crosswise*
*8 3/4 oz. (250 g)*  **leeks**, *cut in half lengthwise*

In a glass bowl, cover anchovies in water and soak for 30 minutes. Remove the outer skin and split the fillet to remove the bone.
In a saucepan over very low heat, cook the garlic cloves until the they soften. Add the anchovy fillets and cook until they are tender and begin to break apart.
Pass the garlic and anchovies through a food mill or blend in a food processor, then pour the mixture (called bagna cauda) into a small heatproof bowl (preferably earthenware) set over a heat burner to keep the sauce hot.
(You can also use a small fondue pot.)
Wash the potatoes, cut into 1-inch chunks and cook until just tender. The other vegetables for dipping can be served raw (or cooked, if desired).
It is important to ensure that the sauce continues to simmer and is not allowed to cool while the vegetables are being dipped.

# TOMATO JELLY
## WITH BURRATA CHEESE AND PESTO

*Preparation time: 30 minutes   Resting time: 2 hours   Difficulty: medium*

### 4 SERVINGS

*2 1/4 lbs. (1 kg)* **ripe tomatoes**, *or about 5 1/2 large*
*3 1/2 oz. (100 g)* **burrata cheese**
*4-5* **gelatin sheets**
**Pesto** *to taste*
**Salt and pepper** *to taste*

*FOR THE PESTO*
*1 cup (15 g)* **packed basil leaves**, *or about 30 leaves*
*1/3 cup (30 g)* **Parmigiano-Reggiano cheese**, *grated*
*3 tbsp. (20 g)* **Pecorino cheese**, *grated*
*1 tbsp. (8 g)* **pine nuts**
*1/3 cup plus 2 tbsp. (100 ml)* **extra-virgin olive oil**, *preferably Ligurian*
*1/2 clove* **garlic**

Wash and dry the basil for the pesto. Combine basil, garlic, Parmigiano-Reggiano, Pecorino, and pine nuts in a mortar and crush them all together. Transfer to a larger bowl and gradually whisk in olive oil until the mixture is creamy and emulsified.

Peel the tomatoes and remove the seeds. Pass them through a food mill or purée them and season them with salt and pepper to taste.

Heat part of the tomato purée in a pan. Soak the gelatin in cold water, add it to the pan and let it dissolve. Add the rest of the tomato purée and pour it into glasses. Refrigerate for at least 2 hours.

Once the jelly sets, top with burrata and pesto. Serve chilled.

# SUN-DRIED-TOMATO
## AND CAPER LOAF

*Preparation time: 15 minutes*   *Cooking time: 35-40 minutes*   *Difficulty: easy*

### 4 SERVINGS

*3 large*  **eggs**
*2 tbsp. (30 ml)*  **extra-virgin olive oil**
*1/3 cup plus 1 1/2 tbsp. (100 ml)*  **milk**
*1 2/3 cups (200 g)*  **all-purpose flour**
*1/4 oz. (7 g)*  **active dry yeast**
*1 cup (100 g)*  **Pecorino cheese**, *grated*
*3 1/2 oz. (100 g)*  **sun-dried tomatoes**
*3 tbsp. (25 g)*  **capers**, *coarsely chopped*
*1 tbsp. (5 g)*  **fresh oregano**, *chopped*
**Salt and pepper** *to taste*
**Butter and flour** *for pan*

Heat oven to 360°F (180°C).
Beat the eggs with the oil and milk, then season with salt and pepper.
Add the flour and yeast, then mix together. Stir in the Pecorino, capers, sun-dried tomatoes, and oregano.
Butter a loaf pan, dust it with with flour and fill it three-quarters full with the batter. Bake for 35 to 40 minutes.

# CAPRESE SALAD

*Preparation time: 15 minutes   Difficulty: easy*

## 4 SERVINGS

8 3/4 oz. (250 g)  **mozzarella cheese** (preferably buffalo-milk mozzarella)
12 oz. (350 g)  **tomatoes**
2 tbsp. (30 ml)  **extra-virgin olive oil**
4  **fresh basil leaves**
**Salt** to taste

Slice the mozzarella and tomatoes and season with a little salt.
Place slices of tomato and mozzarella alternately on a serving dish and decorate with basil leaves.
Drizzle with extra-virgin olive oil and serve.

# OLIVE CROISSANTS

*Preparation time: 1 hour  Rising time: 1 1/2 hours*
*Cooking time: 20 minutes  Difficulty: high*

## 4 SERVINGS

*FOR THE DOUGH*
*4 cups (500 g)* **all-purpose flour**
*1 large* **egg**, *lightly beaten and at*
*room temperature*
*1 tbsp. plus 2 tsp. (20 g)* **sugar**
*1 tbsp. (8.5 g)* **active dry yeast**
*1 cup (250 ml)* **lukewarm water**
*2 tsp. (12 g)* **salt**

*2 tbsp. (25 g)* **unsalted butter**,
*softened, plus more for plastic wrap*

*FOR THE FILLING AND GARNISH*
*2 1/8 oz. (60 g)* **black olive paste**
*1 large* **egg**, *lightly beaten and at*
*room temperature*

Put the flour onto a clean work surface and make a well in the center. Add the sugar and the egg to the well. Dissolve the yeast in the water. Gradually pour the yeast mixture into the well, slowly incorporating the wet ingredients into the flour until a loose dough starts to form, and then begin to knead. Work in the butter and lastly add the salt. Continue kneading until the dough is soft, smooth and elastic. Cover the dough with a sheet of lightly greased plastic and let it rise in a warm place for about 30 minutes.

Roll out the dough with a rolling pin on a floured work surface to a thickness of about 1/8 inch (3 mm). Spread the black olive paste over the surface, using a flexible spatula, and cut the dough into isosceles triangles. Roll them up from the base of the triangle to make the croissants. Arrange them on a greased baking sheet and let them rise again, covered with lightly greased plastic wrap, until doubled in size, about 1 hour.

Brush the surface of the croissants with the beaten egg to make them golden brown. Bake in the oven at 425°F (215°C) for 20 minutes, or until golden.

# SPINACH PIE

*Preparation time: 1 hour    Cooking time: 30 minutes    Difficulty: medium*

## 4 SERVINGS

*FOR THE DOUGH*
1 cup (150 g)  **all-purpose flour**
1 tbsp. (15 g)  **unsalted butter**
3/4 tsp. (5 g)  **salt**
**Sparkling water**, *as needed*

*FOR THE FILLING*
17 1/2 oz. (500 g)  **chard**, *washed and chopped*
8 3/4 oz. (250 g)  **spinach**, *washed and chopped*

1 1/2 oz. (40 g)  **lard** *or bacon fat*
2/3 cup (100 g)  **onion**, *finely chopped*
1 clove  **garlic**, *finely chopped*
1 3/4 oz. (50 g)  **Parmigiano-Reggiano cheese**, *grated, or about  1/2 cup*
**Breadcrumbs**, *as needed*
**Nutmeg** *to taste*
**Salt** *to taste*
**Olive oil** *for pan*

Whisk together the flour and salt. Cut the butter into the flour until the texture is pebbly. Add sparkling water as needed just until the dough begins to form. Turn the dough out onto a floured work surface and knead the dough until it is smooth. Let the dough rest, covered with lightly greased plastic wrap, for 10 minutes.
Heat 3/4 of the lard. Sauté the chard and spinach until wilted. Squeeze out excess water; drain. Add the onion and garlic, and sauté. Add the salt, nutmeg, the Parmigiano-Reggiano, and enough breadcrumbs for a firm filling.
Divide the dough into two balls, one slightly larger. Roll out the larger ball to 1/8 inch thick; line a lightly oiled baking pan with dough. Spread with the filling. Roll out second ball to 1/8 inch thick. Place on top of filling.
Scatter top with small bits of lard and pierce dough all over with a fork.
Bake in the oven at 390°F (200°C) for about 30 minutes.

# BROCCOLI FLAN

*Preparation time: 30 minutes    Cooking time: 40 minutes    Difficulty: easy*

## 4 SERVINGS

9 oz. (250 g) **broccoli**, florets and stems
2/3 cup (150 ml) **cream**
1 oz. (25 g) **Parmigiano-Reggiano cheese**, grated, or about 1/4 cup
3 large **eggs**
2 tsp. (10 g) **unsalted butter**
**Salt and pepper** to taste

*FOR THE SAUCE*
2 **salted anchovies**
2 tbsp. (30 ml) **extra-virgin olive oil**

Heat oven to 300°F (150°C). Boil a medium pan of salted water. Add the broccoli and cook until the stems are tender when tested with a fork. Refresh in iced water, then drain.

Put the broccoli in a blender, then add the cream, Parmigiano-Reggiano, and eggs. Blend until the mixture is smooth. Season with salt and pepper.

Butter individual ramekins and fill with the broccoli mixture. Place ramekins in a hot water bath (bain-marie) or a roasting pan filled with hot water to reach halfway up ramekins and bake in the oven for about 40 minutes.

Meanwhile, prepare the anchovy sauce. Desalt and fillet the anchovies. Place anchovies and oil in a blender, and blend until smooth.

When flans are cooked, remove them from water bath and let them cool for a few minutes. Invert the ramekins over serving plates to remove flans. Garnish with anchovy sauce.

# FRICIULE (FRIED DOUGH)

*Preparation time: 20 minutes   Rising time: 1 hour*
*Cooking time: 5 minutes   Difficulty: medium*

## 4 SERVINGS

*4 cups (500 g)* **soft wheat flour** *(preferably Italian type "00" flour)*
*1 cup plus 2 1/2 tbsp. (275 ml)* **lukewarm water**
*1 tbsp. (8.5 g)* **active dry yeast**
*1 2/3 tsp. (10 g)* **salt**
*2 tsp. (10 ml)* **extra-virgin olive oil**
**Vegetable oil** *for frying*

*FOR THE TOPPING*
*2 tbsp.* **lard** *or bacon fat*
*1 sprig* **fresh rosemary**, *chopped, for garnish*

Put the flour on a clean work surface and make a well in the center. Dissolve the yeast in the water. Pour the yeast mixture, oil, and salt into the well, incorporating them into the flour a little at a time. Knead the dough until it is smooth and elastic.
Let the dough rise, covered with a sheet of lightly greased plastic wrap, in a warm room until it has doubled in size, about one hour.
On a lightly floured surface, roll out the dough with a rolling pin to a thickness of about 1/25 inch (1 mm). Cut the dough into rectangles of about 2 x 3 inches (5 x 8 cm).
Heat 1/2 inch of oil in a large skillet until hot and shimmering. Fry the dough, in batches, until lightly browned on both sides. Season with salt. Before serving, place a thin slice of lard or bacon fat and a pinch of rosemary on each friciula.

# BLINI-STYLE PANCAKES

*Preparation time: 10 minutes    Cooking time: 5 minutes    Difficulty: easy*

## 4 SERVINGS

*4 large*  **eggs**
*1 bunch*  **combined chives, parsley, mint, chervil** *(about 1/3 cup)*
*1/3 cup plus 1 tbsp. (50 g)*  **all-purpose flour**
*3 1/2 tbsp. (50 ml)*  **milk**
*1 1/2 tbsp. (25 ml)*  **extra-virgin olive oil**
**Salt and pepper** *to taste*

Wash, throughly dry, and chop the herbs.
In a bowl, whisk together the eggs, chopped herbs, flour, milk, salt, and pepper until smooth.
Heat a crêpe pan or a small nonstick skillet over medim-low. For each pancake coat skillet with a little oil and drop in a spoonful of the batter. Cook until tiny bubbles form on the surface and edges are lightly browned, about 2 minutes. Immediately flip blini and cook until golden, about 1 to 2 minutes more. Transfer to a plate and cover with foil to keep warm.
Repeat to make a total of 4 pancakes. If you prefer smaller pancakes, divide the batter to make 8 blini.

# CRISPY FISH FRITTERS

*Preparation time: 10 minutes   Cooking time: 10 minutes   Difficulty: easy*

## 4 SERVINGS

*1 lb. (500 g)* **small fish such as anchovies,** *sardines, or herring, filleted (or packed unsalted)*
*10 1/2 oz. (300 g)* **flour,** *or about 2 2/5 cups*
*2/3 cup (150 ml)* **water**
*1 small bunch of* **parsley,** *chopped*
*3 tbsp. (40 ml)* **extra-virgin olive** *oil for frying*
**Salt and black** *pepper to taste*

In a large bowl, mix together the flour, water, salt, parsley and pepper
to form a batter.
Wash the fish thoroughly but gently. Place in the bowl of batter and stir to coat.
Heat the olive oil in a skillet on medium to high until oil is hot and shimmering.
Carefully place spoonfuls of the battered fish into the hot oil and fry for 2 to 3
minutes, or until the fritters are crisp and golden brown.
(Cook in batches if you prefer.)
Remove fritters from the skillet with a slotted spoon and place on a serving plate
lined with paper towels to remove excess oil.
Sprinkle with salt to taste and serve hot.

# POTATO CAKE

*Preparation time: 1 hour   Cooking time: 30 minutes   Difficulty: easy*

## 4 SERVINGS

*2 lbs. (800 g)* **potatoes**
*2 oz. (40 g)* **Parmigiano-Reggiano cheese**, *grated, or about 1/3 cup plus 1 tbsp.*
*5 oz. (150 g)* **Neapolitan salami**
*5 oz. (150 g)* **cooked ham**
*9 oz. (250 g)* **mozzarella cheese**, *diced*
*1 tbsp.* **parsley**, *chopped*
*2 large* **eggs**
*1 1/2 tbsp. (20 g)* **unsalted butter**
*2 oz. (50 g)* **fresh breadcrumbs**, *or about 1 cup*
**Salt and pepper** *to taste*

Heat oven to 340°F (170°C). Wash the potatoes and boil them in a pot
of salted water, skins on, until tender, about 15 to 20 minutes. Drain potatoes
and let them cool completely.

Meanwhile, dice the salami and ham.

Peel potatoes and mash them in a large bowl. Add the eggs, Parmigiano-Reggiano
salami, ham and mozzarella. Add salt, a sprinkling of pepper and the parsley.
Butter a baking dish or four individual ramekins. Sprinkle bottom of baking
dishes with half the breadcrumbs and fill with the potato mixture. Level the
surface, sprinkle with remaining breadcrumbs and dot with butter. (Alternatively
instead of mixing the ingredients, you can layer them: potatoes, ham, salami and
mozzarella, finishing with a layer of potato.) Bake for about 30 minutes.

# PARMIGIANO-REGGIANO BUNS

*Preparation time: 1 hour   Rising time: 1 1/2 hours*
*Cooking time: 20 minutes   Difficulty: high*

## 4 SERVINGS

*FOR THE DOUGH*
4 cups (500 g) **pastry flour**
1 **egg**
1 tbsp. plus 2 tsp. (20 g) **sugar**
1 tbsp. (8.5 g) **active dry yeast**
1 cup (250 ml) **lukewarm water**
2 tsp. (12 g) **salt**
2 tbsp. (25 g) **unsalted butter**, softened

*FOR THE FILLING*
2 oz. (60 g) **Parmigiano-Reggiano cheese**, grated, or about 2/3 cup
1 **egg**, lightly beaten

Put the flour on a clean work surface and make a well in the center. Add the sugar and egg to the well. Dissolve the yeast in the water. Add the yeast mixture, gradually, incorporating the ingredients into the flour. When the dough begins to form, add the butter and, lastly, the salt. Knead the dough until it is smooth and elastic.

Cover the dough with a sheet of lightly greased plastic and let it rest for about 30 minutes. Butter a baking sheet.

On a lightly floured work surface, roll out the dough to about 1/8 inch (3 mm) thick. Brush the surface with some of the beaten egg and cover with the Parmigiano-Reggiano. Roll the sheet of pastry evenly into a rope and slice it into 3/4-inch (2 cm) lengths.

Transfer to a baking sheet and let buns rise again, until they double in size (1 hour). Brush the surface with remaining beaten egg and bake at 400°F (200°C) for about 20 minutes.

# BEEF TARTARE SALAD

*Preparation time: 20 minutes    Difficulty: easy*

## 4 SERVINGS

*10 2/3 oz. (300 g)* **beef tenderloin**
*1/3 cup (80 ml)* **extra-virgin olive oil**
*1 clove* **garlic**
*2* **salt-packed anchovies**
*Juice from 1* **lemon**
*2/3 oz. (20 g)* **Parmigiano-Reggiano cheese**, *shaved*
*3 1/2 oz. (100 g)* **celery**
**Truffle** *to taste (optional)*
**Salt and pepper** *to taste*

Chop the beef tenderloin into a small dice. Place the meat in a bowl and season it with salt and pepper. Desalt, debone and chop the anchovies, and add them to the meat with the whole peeled clove of garlic, olive oil and a little lemon juice. Let set for 5 to 10 minutes and then remove the garlic.
Use a steel press to flatten the meat (or form into individual mounds or patties to serve). Garnish it with the sliced celery, the shaved Parmigiano-Reggiano and thin slices of truffle, if available. Complete by grinding some pepper and drizzling a little olive oil over the tartare.

# WARM SPELT SALAD
## WITH SHRIMP

*Preparation time: 30 minutes    Cooking time: 40 minutes    Difficulty: easy*

### 4 SERVINGS

*3/4 cup (150 g)* **spelt**
*12* **shrimp**, peeled (leave tail segment intact) and deveined
*3 1/2 oz. (100 g)* **carrots**, or about 2 small, cut into a fine dice
*3 1/2 oz. (100 g)* **zucchini**, or about 1 small, cut into a fine dice
*3 1/2 oz. (100 g)* **tomato**, or about 1/2 large
*1/3 cup (50 g)* **peas**
*1 3/4 oz. (50 g)* **red onion**, or about 1 small
*1 tsp.* **minced parsley**
*A few* **basil leaves**
*3 tbsp. plus 2 tsp. (50 ml)* **extra-virgin olive oil**
**Salt** *to taste*

Bring a small saucepan of salted water to a boil. Add the peas and cook them until just tender. Drain and run the peas under cold water. Drain again. Heat 1 tablespoon plus 2 teaspoons oil in a skillet over medium heat. Add the onion and cook until tender. Add the diced zucchini and carrots and season with salt and pepper. Cook until lightly browned but not softened.
Peel the tomato, remove the seeds and dice it. Boil the spelt in salted water, strain it and put it in a bowl. Add the cooked vegetables, diced tomatoes and basil. Season with olive oil and salt to taste.
Sauté the shrimp in a bit of oil until cooked through and browned. Serve them with the spelt salad.

# FRIED MOZZARELLA CAPRESE

*Preparation time: 25 minutes    Cooking time: 5 minutes    Difficulty: easy*

## 4 SERVINGS

*1/2 lb. (250 g)  **mozzarella cheese***
*2 cups (275 g)  **dried breadcrumbs***
*3/4 lb. (350 g)  **vine-ripened tomatoes**, or about 2 large*
*1/3 cup plus 1 tbsp. (50 g)  **all-purpose flour***
*3 large  **eggs**, lightly beaten*
*4 leaves  **basil***
***Salt** to taste*
***Olive oil** for frying*

Slice the mozzarella and tomatoes to equal thickness.
Stack four alternating layers of tomato and mozzarella, inserting basil leaves
between layers. Wrap each stack in parchment paper to absorb excess liquid.
Place flour in one bowl, the beaten eggs in another bowl and the breadcrumbs
in a third bowl. Remove parchment from stacks and dredge each stack in flour,
then dip in the beaten egg and coat with breadcrumbs. Once more, dip the
stack in the egg and coat in breadcrumbs, shaking off excess.
Heat 1/2 inch of oil in a large skillet until hot and shimmering. Using a slotted
spoon, carefully transfer the stacks to the hot oil and fry for about 30 seconds.
Turn with the slotted spoon to fry on the other side for 30 seconds more.
Remove stacks with the slotted spoon and transfer them to paper towels to
absorb excess oil.
Sprinkle with salt and serve.

# SUN-DRIED-TOMATO
## AND CAPER TWISTS

*Preparation time: 1 hour   Rising time: 1 1/2 hours*
*Cooking time: 20 minutes   Difficulty: easy*

### 4 SERVINGS

*FOR THE DOUGH*
4 cups (500 g) **all-purpose flour**
1 large **egg**
1 tbsp. plus 2 tsp. (20 g) **sugar**
1 tbsp. (8.5 g) **active dry yeast**
1 cup (250 ml) **lukewarm water**
2 tsp. (12 g) **salt**
2 tbsp. (25 g) **unsalted butter**, softened

*FOR THE FILLING*
2 oz. (60 g) **sun-dried tomatoes**, chopped
3/4 cup (150 g) **salted capers**, rinsed and patted dry
1 **egg**, lightly beaten
Chopped **fresh oregano** to taste

Dissolve the yeast in the water. Put the flour on a clean work surface and make a well in the center. Add the sugar and egg to the well. Add the yeast mixture gradually, incorporating the ingredients into the flour. When the dough begins to form, add the butter and, lastly, the salt. Knead the dough until it is smooth and elastic. Cover the dough with a sheet of lightly greased plastic wrap and let rise in a warm place for about 30 minutes.

On a lightly floured surface, roll out the dough with a rolling pin to 1/8 inch (3 mm) thick. Brush the surface with some of the beaten egg and sprinkle with the chopped sun-dried tomatoes, the capers, and oregano to taste.

Butter a baking sheet. Fold the sheet of dough in half to enclose the filling, and cut it into strips of 1 to 1 1/4 inches (2.5 to 3 cm) in length. Twist the strips and place them on the baking sheet. Let rise again until doubled in size, about 1 hour. Brush surface with the rest of the egg. Bake in the oven at 400°F (200°C) for 20 minutes, or until golden brown.

# ASCOLI-STYLE OLIVES

*Preparation time: 1 hour   Cooking time: 4 minutes   Difficulty: medium*

## 4 SERVINGS

20 **very large green olives** (tender ones
from Ascoli, if available), pitted
1 3/4 oz. (50 g) **lean pork**, finely diced
1 3/4 oz. (50 g) **lean veal**, finely diced
1 3/4 oz. (50 g) **chicken breast**, finely diced
1 **chicken liver**, diced
1 tbsp. plus 1 tsp. (20 ml) **extra-virgin
olive oil**
3 tbsp. plus 1 tsp. (50 ml) **white wine**

1 oz. (25 g) **Parmigiano-Reggiano
cheese**, grated, or about 1/4 cup
1/3 cup plus 1 tbsp. (50 g) **all-purpose flour**
2 large **eggs** lightly beaten, plus 1 egg
yolk
1 cup (150 g) **dried breadcrumbs**
**Nutmeg** to taste
**Cinnamon** to taste
**Salt and pepper** to taste
**Vegetable oil** for frying, as needed

Pit the olives with a small knife (or an olive pitter), if necessary, and soak them in
lukewarm water for 10 minutes. Drain.
To prepare the filling, heat the olive oil in a skillet over medium heat and sauté
the diced pork, veal, chicken and chicken liver. Season the mixture with salt and
pepper. Add the wine and continue cooking over medium heat for about 10
minutes, adding a few tablespoons of water if it becomes too dry.
Once cooked, let the mixture cool and then chop finely. Season it with pepper
and a pinch of cinnamon and nutmeg. Add the egg yolk and the Parmigiano-
Reggiano and mix well. Stuff the olives, maintaining their original shape.
Place the flour in one bowl, the beaten eggs in another and the breadcrumbs in
a third bowl. Dip olives first in the flour, then in the eggs and, lastly, in the
breadcrumbs. Heat 1/2 inch of oil in a large skillet until shimmering. Using a
slotted spoon, place olives in oil and fry until lightly browned on all sides.
Transfer to paper towels to drain excess oil. Serve warm.

# PANZANELLA

*Preparation time: 15 minutes    Difficulty: easy*

## 4 TO 6 SERVINGS

*2 1/4 lb. (1 kg)* **rustic Tuscan bread**,
*preferably day-old*
*1 oz. (30 g)* **anchovy fillets**, *finely chopped*
*7 oz. (200 g)* **tomatoes, diced**, *or
about 2 medium*
*4 oz. (120 g)* **seedless cucumber**,
*diced, or about 1 small*
*5 1/3 oz. (150 g)* **red onions**, *diced, or
about 2 small*
*9 oz. (250 g)* **bell peppers**, *about 2
medium*

*1 clove* **garlic**, *minced*
*1 tbsp. (10 g)* **capers**, *well rinsed and
finely chopped*
*20* **fresh basil** *leaves*
*1 tbsp. (15 ml)* **red wine vinegar**
*1/4 cup plus 2 tbsp. (80 ml)* **extra-
virgin olive oil**
*1/2 tsp. (3 g)* **salt**
**Black pepper** *to taste*

Cut the bread into 3/4-inch cubes (2 cm) cubes, leaving the crust on.
In a large bowl, combine the garlic, anchovies and capers with the salt, pepper,
vinegar and oil. Mix well.
Add the diced cucumber, onions, and peppers along with the bread to the
garlic/anchovy mixture. Mix again, making sure everything is coated
with dressing, and season with salt and pepper to taste. Add a few leaves
of basil to garnish.
Panzanella is even tastier if you make it the day before and refrigerate
it overnight to let all the flavors meld.

# POTATO TORTE

*Preparation time: 30 minutes   Rising time: 30 minutes*
*Cooking time: 20 minutes   Difficulty: medium*

## 4 SERVINGS

### FOR THE DOUGH
*1/8 lb. (65 g)* **boiled potatoes**, *about 1 medium*
*1 cup (125 g)* **flour**
*2 large* **egg yolks**
*1 1/4 tbsp. (18 g)* **unsalted butter**, *softened*
*3/4 tsp. (2 g)* **active dry yeast**
*1/2 tsp. (2 g)* **fine salt**
*1 1/2 tsp. (10 g)* **butter** *for greasing the pan*

### FOR THE FILLING
*1/3 lb. (150 g)* **ricotta cheese**
*3/4 oz. (20 g)* **bacon**, *cooked and dice*
*3/4 oz. (20 g)* **Gruyère cheese**, *dice*
*1/2 oz. (15 g)* **Parmigiano-Reggiano cheese**, *grated*
**Parsley**, *chopped*
**Salt and pepper** *to taste*

Butter a pie plate and set aside. Boil the potatoes and fry the bacon. Mash th
boiled potatoes, or press through a potato ricer into a bowl. Put the potatoes
a clean work surface and make a well in the center. Put the flour, egg yolks,
butter, yeast and, lastly, the fine salt in the well. Knead the ingredients togethe
gradually until you obtain a smooth, soft dough. Divide dough into two disks
In a large bowl, mix the ricotta with the salt, pepper, Parmigiano-Reggiano,
chopped parsley, bacon and Gruyère.
On a lightly floured surface, roll out 1 disk to about 1/4 inch (6 mm) thick. Fit th
dough into the pie plate. Add the filling, spreading evenly.
Roll out second disk to 1/4 inch (6 mm) thick. Place on top of filling. Trim off
excess dough and seal the edges of the crusts, using the tines of a fork. Prick t
surface with the fork to allow steam to escape.
Let the torte rise, lightly covered in greased plastic wrap for at least 30 minute
Bake at 320°F (160°C) for about 20 minutes. Let cool slightly before serving.

# POTATOES
## WITH CASTELMAGNO CHEESE AND EGGS

*Preparation time: 30 minutes   Cooking time: 10 minutes   Difficulty: easy*

### 4 SERVINGS

4 **medium  potatoes**, peeled
4 large  **eggs**
2 oz. (60 g)  **Castelmagno** or Gorgonzola cheese
2 tbsp. (30 g)  **unsalted butter**
**Salt and pepper** to taste

Boil whole potatoes in a pot of lightly salted boiling water for about 15 minutes.
Let cool, and leave potatoes whole.
Heat the oven to 350°F (180°).
Holding the potato lengthwise, scoop out a portion of the interior,
making a small cavity.
Arrange the potatoes in a baking pan lined with parchment paper. Break an egg
into the cavity of each potato, then season with salt, pepper and a dab of butter.
Sprinkle crumbled cheese over the potatoes and bake for 10 minutes.

# STUFFED PEPPERS
## WITH MONKFISH

*Preparation time: 50 minutes*  *Cooking time: 15 minutes*  *Difficulty: easy*

### 4 SERVINGS

*2* **red bell peppers**
*About 3/4 lb. (350 g)* **monkfish**
**Salt and pepper** *to taste*
**Fresh herbs**, *for garnish (optional)*

Heat the oven to 375°F (190°C). In a large shallow pan, roast the peppers for 20 minutes. Turn them every 5 minutes so they do not become soft and overcooked. Transfer peppers to a bowl and allow to cool. Peel them, removing stems, seeds and ribs. Cut peppers into wide strips.
Decrease oven temperature to 300°F (150°C).
Clean the monkfish, debone, and slice it lengthwise to get 2 long fillets just over 1 inch (3 cm) wide.
Season them with salt and pepper. Lay them over the pepper slices and roll them up. Wrap a piece of aluminum foil around each and bake for about 15 minutes.
Let pepper rolls cool slightly, then slice them into rounds and serve garnished with fresh herbs, if desired.

# MESSINA FRIED PIZZA

*Preparation time: 30 minutes   Rising time: 1 1/2 hours*
*Cooking time: 5 minutes   Difficulty: medium*

## 4 SERVINGS

*FOR THE DOUGH*
2 1/3 cups (350 g) **all-purpose flour**
1 cup (150 g) **semolina flour**
1 cup plus 2 tbsp. (270 ml) **lukewarm water**
1 3/4 oz. (50 g) **lard**
1 tbsp. plus 3/4 tsp. (10 g) **active dry
yeast**
1 1/2 tsp. (10 g) **salt**
**Vegetable oil** for frying, as needed

*FOR THE FILLING*
1 head **escarole**
6 **anchovies**, desalted or in oil, chopped
10 **cherry tomatoes**, quartered
3 1/2 oz. (100 g) **Caciocavallo** or
provolone cheese, diced
2 tbsp. (30 ml) **extra-virgin olive oil**
**Salt and pepper** to taste

Mix both flours and put on a clean work surface. Make a well in the center. Dissolve
the salt in 3 tbsp. (50 ml) of water. Dissolve yeast in remaining water. Put the lard in
the well. Gradually add the yeast mixture, then the salt mixture into the dough.
Continue kneading the dough until smooth and elastic. Let the dough rise, covered
with a sheet of lightly greased plastic, until it doubles in size, about 1 hour.
Meanwhile, prepare the filling. Chop the escarole into strips and put it in a bowl. Add
oil, salt and pepper and toss. Add the tomatoes, cheese and anchovies; mix well.
Divide dough into balls of 3 1/2 oz. (100 g) each. Let them rise, covered with plastic
wrap, for 30 minutes. Roll them out into discs about 1/8 inch (3 mm) thick. Spread
the filling over half the surface of each disc. Fold in half and seal the edges.
Heat 1/2 inch of oil in a large skillet until shimmering. Fry the pizzas, a few at a time,
until they are golden brown (about 5 minutes). Remove to paper towels to remove
excess oil. Season with a pinch of salt.

# MINI PIZZAS

*Preparation time: 30 minutes    Cooking time: 13 minutes    Difficulty: easy*

## 4 SERVINGS

*10 oz. (300 g)*  **puff pastry**, *or about 1 sheet*
*9 oz. (250 g)*  **assorted tomatoes**
*1 3/4 oz. (50 g)*  **Scamorza** *or Emmental cheese, diced*
*1/2 oz. (15 g)*  **anchovy fillets**
*1 oz. (25 g)*  **pitted olives**, *or about 6 large, chopped*
*1 tbsp. (10 g)*  **capers**
**Fresh oregano**
**Salt** *to taste*

Preheat the oven to 400°F (200°C). On a clean, lightly floured work surface, roll out the puff pastry to about 1/8 inch (3 mm) thick (about 10 inches square). Cut out 12 small rounds. Put them on a baking sheet lined with parchment paper and prick them with a fork.

Dice the tomatoes (or purée them if you prefer) and sprinkle tomatoes and cheese evenly over the tops of the pizzas.

Garnish with the anchovies, olives and capers as you wish. Sprinkle with a little oregano and a pinch of salt.

Bake for about 13 minutes, or until the cheese is bubbly and the crust is golden brown.

# EGGPLANT FRITTERS

*Preparation time: 1 hour    Cooking time: 5 minutes    Difficulty: easy*

## 4 SERVINGS

*1 lb. (450 g)* **eggplant**, *rinsed, trimmed, and peeled if desired*
*1 large* **egg**
*4 oz. (100 g)* **breadcrumbs**, *or about 3/4 cup*
*1 tsp.* **chopped parsley**
*1 clove* **garlic**
*4* **basil leaves**, *chopped*
*1 3/4 oz. (50 g)* **Pecorino cheese**, *grated*
**Vegetable oil** *for frying, as needed*
**Salt** *to taste*

Cut the eggplant in half, put it into a pot, and cover with water. Bring to a boil,
reduce the heat, and simmer for about 45 minutes. Drain and let cool.
In a large bowl, mix the breadcrumbs, garlic, parsley, basil, cheese, and salt to taste.
Squeeze out the excess liquid from the eggplants, then add them to the bowl
with the breadcrumbs. Add the egg and mash the mixture until well
blended and smooth.
Shape the mixture into slightly elongated, fairly flat balls. Heat about 1/2 inch
of oil in a large pan over medium heat, then fry the eggplant balls until golden
brown on all sides. Transfer to a plate lined with paper towels to drain
briefly before serving.
Serve the fritters hot or cold, garnished with thin strips of eggplant peel, if desired.

# FRIED GREEN TOMATOES

*Preparation time: 15 minutes    Cooking time: 5 minutes    Difficulty: easy*

## 4 SERVINGS

*1 lb. 2 oz. (500 g)* **green tomatoes**, *or about 3 large*
*1/3 cup (50 g)* **all-purpose flour**
*2 large* **eggs**, *beaten*
*1 1/4 cups (150 g)* **breadcrumbs**
*3/4 cup (200 ml)* **extra-virgin olive oil**
**Salt** *to taste*

Wash the tomatoes and cut into 1/4-inch (6 mm) slices.
Put the flour in a bowl, the eggs in a second bowl and the breadcrumbs in a
third bowl. Dip the tomatoes in flour to coat, then in the eggs, and finally
in the breadcrumbs.
Heat the oil in a large pan over medium heat. Add the coated tomatoes and f
for about 5 minutes, flipping them with a spatula halfway through. Transfer to
plate lined with paper towels to drain briefly. Sprinkle with salt and serve.

# GORGONZOLA ROLLS

*Preparation time: 1 hour   Rising time: 1 1/2 hours*
*Cooking time: 20 minutes   Difficulty: high*

## 4 SERVINGS

### FOR THE DOUGH
*4 cups (500 g)* **all-purpose flour**
*1 large* **egg**
*1 tbsp. plus 2 tsp. (20 g)* **sugar**
*1 tbsp. (8.5 g)* **active dry yeast**
*1 cup (250 ml)* **lukewarm water**
*2 tsp. (12 g)* **salt**
*2 tbsp. (25 g)* **unsalted butter**

### FOR THE FILLING
*4 1/4 oz. (150 g)* **Gorgonzola cheese**,
*crumbled*
*1 3/4 oz. (50 g)* **shelled walnuts**
*1* **egg**, *lightly beaten*

Put the flour on a clean work surface and make a well in the center. Add the sugar and egg to the well. Dissolve the yeast in the water. Add the yeast mixture gradually, incorporating the ingredients into the flour a little at a time. When the dough begins to form, add the butter and, lastly, the salt. Knead the dough until it is smooth and elastic. Let the dough rise in a warm place, covered with lightly greased plastic wrap, for about 30 minutes. Meanwhile, preheat the oven to 400°F (200°C), and butter a baking sheet.

On a clean, lightly floured work surface, roll out the dough to about 1/8 inch (3 mm) thick. Cut the dough into 2-by-6-inch (5-by-15-cm) rectangles. Place a morsel of Gorgonzola and a couple of walnut pieces in the center of each. Fold rectangles in half, wrapping the dough around itself to form a package. Seal edges.

Transfer to the prepared baking sheet and let buns rise again, covered with greased plastic wrap, until they are doubled in size (about 1 hour). Brush the surface with the remaining beaten egg and bake for about 20 minutes, or until golden brown.

# PARMIGIANO-REGGIANO SOUFFLÉ

*Preparation time: 20 minutes    Cooking time: 20 minutes    Difficulty: easy*

## 4 SERVINGS

*3 oz. (90 g)* **Parmigiano-Reggiano cheese**, *grated, or about 1 cup*
*1 cup (250 ml)* **fresh cream**
*1 1/4 tbsp. (10 g)* **cornstarch**
*1 tbsp.* **lukewarm milk**
*2 large* **eggs**, *beaten*
*3/4 tbsp. (10 g)* **butter**
**Salt and pepper** *to taste*

Preheat the oven to 300°F (150°C).
Heat the cream in a saucepan over low. Dissolve the cornstarch in the milk, the
whisk into the cream. Let cool for a few minutes.
Whisk beaten eggs into the cream mixture, then whisk in the Parmigiano-Reggian
Butter a soufflé dish or individual ramekins and transfer batter to them.
Place baking dishes in a bain-marie (or water bath: a roasting pan and fill with
enough hot water to reach halfway up the baking dish or ramekins). Bake for
about 20 minutes, or until soufflé is puffed and golden brown.

# CASTELMAGNO SOUFFLÉ

*Preparation time: 30 minutes   Cooking time: 18 minutes   Difficulty: easy*

## 4 SERVINGS

*1/2 cup (100 g)* **unsalted butter**
*1/3 cup (40 g)* **all-purpose flour**
*1 cup (250 ml)* **lukewarm milk**
*4 large* **eggs**, *separated*
*5 oz. (150 g)* **Castelmagno** *or Gorgonzola cheese*
*1/4 cup (30 g)* **breadcrumbs**
**Salt and pepper** *to taste*
**Nutmeg** *to taste*

Preheat the oven to 350°F (176°C).
Melt the butter in a saucepan over medium heat. Whisk in the flour, then the
milk, until smooth, and cook about 3 minutes.
Into flour mixture whisk salt, pepper and a pinch of grated nutmeg.
Remove from heat to let mixture cool slightly, about 1 minute.
Whisk in egg yolks 1 at a time, as well as the crumbled Castelmagno or
Gorgonzola cheese.
With an electric mixer, in a separate bowl, beat the egg whites until stiff but no
dry. Fold them gently into the egg mixture.
Transfer the batter to individual buttered ramekins and sprinkle with
breadcrumbs. Place ramekins in a bain-marie (or water bath: a roasting pan and
fill with enough hot water to reach halfway up the baking dish or ramekins). Bak
for about 18 minutes, or until soufflés are puffed and golden brown.

# ARANCINI WITH BEEF
## (RICE BALLS)

*Preparation time: 1 hour    Cooking time: 5 minutes    Difficulty: medium*

### 4 SERVINGS

1 1/2 cups (300 g) **Arborio rice**
1 3/4 oz. (50 g) **onion**, *minced*
3 1/2 tbsp. (50 ml) **extra-virgin olive oil**
2/3 cup (150 ml) **white wine**
1 cup (200 g) **peeled tomatoes**, *finely chopped*
3 1/2 oz. (100 g) **ground beef**
3 pints (1.5 l) **beef stock**
3/4 cup plus 1 tbsp. (80 g) **Parmigiano-Reggiano cheese**, *grated*

2 tbsp. (30 g) **unsalted butter**
3 1/2 oz. (100 g) **mozzarella cheese**, *finely diced*
2 large **eggs**
1/3 cup plus 1 tbsp. (50 g) **all-purpose flour**
1 cups (150 g) **breadcrumbs**
**Salt and pepper** *to taste*
**Vegetable oil for frying**, *as needed*

Season the ground beef with salt and pepper. Heat half the olive oil in a skillet and sauté the ground beef with half the wine for 10 minutes. Bring the beef stock to a boil in a saucepan. In another skillet, using the remaining oil, sauté the minced onion. Add the rice and toast it, stirring constantly. Add remaining wine and cook until wine evaporates. Add tomatoes and cook for 16-18 minutes, gradually adding the boiling beef stock. When the rice is almost cooked, add the ground beef. When it is al dente, remove from heat and stir in butter and Parmigiano-Reggiano. Spread rice mixture evenly in a baking pan; let it cool. Add the mozzarella and form it into small, 3-3 1/4 in. (8-9 cm), balls.
Put flour, beaten eggs, and breadcrumbs into separate bowls. Dredge rice balls first in flour, then egg, then breadcrumbs. Heat oil until it is shimmering. Fry the rice balls until browned. Using a slotted spoon, transfer to paper towels to drain. Serve warm.

# BACON TARTLETS

*Preparation time: 1 hour*  *Cooking time: 15 minutes*  *Difficulty: easy*

## 4 SERVINGS

*1/4 lb. (120 g)* **puff pastry**, *or 1 sheet*
*1 3/4 oz. (50 g)* **pancetta** *or thick bacon, diced*
*1/2 lb. (250 g)* **potatoes**
*1/2 cup (125 ml)* **milk**
*1 large* **egg**
*1 sprig* **fresh rosemary**, *chopped*
**Salt and pepper** *to taste*

Scrub the potatoes and boil them, skins on, in a saucepan of of lightly salted water until tender but still firm, about 15 minutes. Drain, cool and peel potatoes, then either dice them or slice into thick rounds.

Preheat oven to 350°F (180°C).

On a clean work surface, roll out the puff pastry to about 1/12 inch (2 mm) thick. Divide into 4 pieces. Line four individual tartlet pans with the puff pastry. Fill the pans with the pancetta and potatoes.

In a bowl, whisk the egg together with the milk, salt, pepper and rosemary. Pour into the tartlet pans, place on a baking sheet, and bake for about 15 minutes or until golden brown.

# EASTER CHEESE BREAD

*Preparation time: 1 1/2 hours   Cooking time: 40 minutes   Difficulty: easy*

## 4 SERVINGS

2 2/3 cups (325 g)  **all-purpose flour**
1 cup plus 3 tbsp. (120 g)  **Pecorino cheese**, grated
2 oz. (50 g)  **Pecorino cheese**, diced, or about 1/2 cup
5 1/2 tbsp. (90 g)  **melted butter**, plus more for pan
1 tbsp. plus 3/4 tsp. (10 g)  **active dry yeast**
1 1/2 tsp. (7 g)  **baking powder**
1/3 cup plus 1 1/2 tbsp. (100 ml)  **lukewarm water**
4 large  **eggs**
1/3 cup plus 2 1/2 tbsp. (50 g)  **breadcrumbs**
**Salt and pepper** to taste

Dissolve yeast in the water.
Whisk together the flour and baking powder. Put the flour mixture on a clean work surface and make a well in the center.
Whisk 3 eggs with salt, pepper, 1 cup of grated cheese and all of diced cheese and mix with the flour. Gradually add the butter and the yeast mixture and begin to knead until dough is smooth and elastic.
Grease one loaf pan or four ramekins and line them with breadcrumbs. Divide dough as needed and fill the pan or ramekins halfway. Let the dough rise until it doubles in size, about 1 hour.
Preheat oven to 350° F (180° C). Beat the remaining 1 egg lightly and brush the dough's surface with it. Sprinkle dough with freshly ground pepper and the remaining grated Pecorino. Bake for about 40 minutes.

# GOAT CHEESE CAKE

*Preparation time: 20 minutes*    *Cooking time: 30 minutes*    *Difficulty: easy*

## 4 SERVINGS

7 oz. (200 g) **puff pastry**, or about 1 sheet
7 oz. (200 g) **tomatoes**, about 2 medium
2 oz. (60 g) **goat cheese** (Caprino, if available)
2/3 cup (150 ml) **lukewarm milk**
1 large **egg**
1 tsp. **cornstarch**
2 1/2 tbsp. (15 g) **Parmigiano-Reggiano cheese**, grated
1 bunch **chives**
**Salt and pepper** to taste

Preheat the oven to 350°F (180°C).
On a clean work surface, roll out the puff pastry to about 1/8 inch (3 mm) thick.
Line a baking pan or 4 ramekins with the pastry.
Slice the tomatoes and the goat cheese. Arrange the sliced tomatoes and goat cheese on the surface of the puff pastry.
Meanwhile, rinse, dry, and chop the chives. In a medium bowl, dissolve the cornstarch into 1/3 cup of the milk. Whisk the egg, the remaining 1/3 cup milk, the Parmigiano-Reggiano, salt, pepper and chives into the cornstarch mixture.
Pour the mixture into the baking pan or divide evenly among ramekins.
Bake for about 25 minutes or until cheese is lightly browned.

# GORGONZOLA CAKE

*Preparation time: 20 minutes   Rising time: 1 hour*
*Cooking time: 40 minutes   Difficulty: medium*

## 4 SERVINGS

*2 large  **eggs***
*5 1/3 oz. (150 g)  **Gorgonzola cheese**, diced*
*1/2 stick (50 g)  **unsalted butter**, melted, plus more for pans*
*1 3/4 cups (215 g)  **all-purpose flour**, plus more for dusting*
*1/4 oz. (6.4 g)  **active dry yeast***
*4 3/4 tbsp. (70 ml)  **lukewarm milk***
***Salt and pepper** to taste*

Put the flour on a clean work surface and make a well in the center.
Whisk together the eggs, salt and pepper in a bowl. Dissolve the yeast
in the lukewarm milk.
To the well, gradually add the egg mixture, the cooled melted butter
and the yeast mixture and begin to knead into a dough. Add 4 1/3 oz. (120g)
of diced Gorgonzola.
Butter and flour 4 ramekins and fill them halfway with the mixture. Cover loosely
with lightly greased plastic wrap and let the dough rise until it has doubled in
size (about 1 hour).
Meanwhile, preheat the oven to at 350 °F (180 °C).
Evenly distribute the remaining Gorgonzola on top of the cakes. Place ramekins
on a baking sheet and bake for about 40 minutes.

# POTATO AND ANCHOVY PIE

*Preparation time: 1 hour   Cooking time: 15 minutes   Difficulty: medium*

## 4 SERVINGS

*1 lb. (400 g)* **potatoes**, *about 3 medium*
*2 1/5 lbs. (1 kg)* **fresh anchovies**
*3 1/2 oz. (100 g)* **breadcrumbs**
*2* **cherry tomatoes**, *chopped*
*1 tbsp.* **chopped parsley**
*1 tbsp. plus 1 tsp. (20 ml)* **extra-virgin olive oil**
*4 1/4 tsp. (20 g)* **butter**
**Salt and pepper**

Clean the anchovies, removing the heads, bones, and innards. Butterfly
the fish, then rinse.
Preheat the oven to 340°F (170°C).
Butter a round baking pan and arrange the first layer of anchovies along the
bottom and edges of the pan.
Peel the potatoes and cut into thin slices using a mandoline, if available. Bring
pot of salted water to a boil. Drop the slices in and cook for 5 minutes then
plunge them into ice water to stop the cooking. Drain well. To the baking pan,
alternate a layer of potatoes with one of breadcrumbs, parsley, anchovies, a
drizzle of extra-virgin olive oil and a pinch of salt and pepper.
Finish with the cherry tomatoes and a drizzle of oil.
Bake for about 15 minutes.
Let pie cool in pan for 5 minutes before unmolding it onto a serving plate.

# MARINATED FRIED EGGS
## IN CARPIONE SAUCE

*Preparation time: 15 minutes   Cooking time: 5 minutes*
*Marinating time: 3-4 hours   Difficulty: easy*

### 4 SERVINGS

4 large **eggs**
5 tsp. (25 g) **unsalted butter**
1 clove **garlic**
5 oz. (150 g) **onion**, or about 1 medium
3 1/2 oz. (100 g) **carrot**, or about 2 small
3 1/2 oz. (100 g) **celery**, or about 2 1/2 medium stalks

1 sprig **fresh sage**
1 sprig **fresh thyme**
2 tbsp. (30 ml) **extra-virgin olive oil**
1 1/4 cups (300 ml) **white wine vinegar**
1 1/4 cups (300 ml) **white wine**
**Salt and pepper** to taste

Wash and peel the vegetables. Wash and pat dry the herbs.
Cut the onions into thin slices and cut the carrots and celery stalks into strips.
In a large skillet, heat olive oil and brown the vegetables lightly, then add the whole clove of garlic and the sprigs of thyme and sage.
Add the wine and vinegar and bring to a boil. Pour in a little water and season with salt. Cook for a 3 to 5 minutes.
Meanwhile, melt the butter in a skillet, and fry the eggs just until the whites have set. Gently flip the eggs and cook the other side. Season with salt and pepper.
Arrange the eggs in a large serving bowl, cover with the hot vegetable mixture and let marinate for several hours. Before serving, drain the eggs.
Serve them cold with mayonnaise and mustard or with pickled vegetables.

# HARD-COOKED EGGS
## IN BALSAMIC VINEGAR

*Preparation time: 5 minutes   Cooking time: 8 minutes*
*Marinating time: 12-24 hours   Difficulty: easy*

### 4 SERVINGS

*4 large* **eggs**
*1 1/2 cups (350 ml)* **balsamic vinegar**

Put the eggs in a saucepan of cold water, with water covering eggs by 1 to 2 inches. Bring the water to a boil over high heat. Reduce heat and simmer for 7 to 8 minutes, according to taste.
Drain the eggs and immediately submerge them in cold water to stop the cooking process (and make them easier to peel). Shell the eggs.
Put the balsamic vinegar in a large bowl. Add peeled hard-cooked eggs to the bowl of vinegar and let marinate for at least 12 hours and up to 24 hours. Drain eggs and serve.

# MARBLED HARD-COOKED EGGS

*Preparation time: 5 minutes   Cooking time: 10 minutes   Difficulty: easy*

## 4 SERVINGS

*4 large* **eggs**

*FOR THE COLORING SOLUTION*
*2 cups (500 ml)* **water**
*5 tsp. (25 ml)* **white vinegar**
**Food coloring** *(in the colors of your choice)*

Put the eggs in a saucepan of cold water, with water covering eggs by 1 to 2 inches. Bring the water to a boil over high heat. Reduce heat and simmer for 6 to 7 minutes, according to taste. Drain the eggs and immediately submerge them in cold water to stop the cooking process. Drain them again. With a spoon lightly tap on the shells to "crack" them without removing them.
In another saucepan, mix water, vinegar, and a few drops of food coloring (depending on the depth of color you desire), and bring it to a boil.
Immerse the eggs in the colored water mixture and cook for another 2 to 3 minutes.
Drain the eggs and let them cool. Peel them before serving.

# VITELLO TONNATO

Preparation time: 40 minutes    Cooking time: 40 minutes    Difficulty: medium

## 4 SERVINGS

### FOR THE MEAT
1 1/3 lbs. (600 g) **boned veal eye round**
1/4 cup plus 2 3/4 tbsp. (100 ml) **extra-virgin olive oil**
1 clove **garlic**, peeled
**Fresh rosemary** and sage to taste, rinsed and patted dry
**Salt** to taste

### FOR THE SAUCE
1/2 cup (100 ml) **white wine**
2 **anchovies in salt**, rinsed and dried
1 oz. (30 g) **day-old bread**
10 tsp. (50 ml) **white wine vinegar**
5 **capers** in salt, soaked and rinsed
8 3/4 oz. (250 g) **tuna in oil**, chopped
3 large **hard-cooked egg yolks**
**Veal or beef stock** as needed

Heat oven to 360°F (180°C)

Salt the veal round and brown it in the oil in a Dutch oven or roasting pan over medium heat, about 4 minutes per side.

Add the garlic and the herbs to the pan. Bake until the meat is medium-rare and an instant-read thermometer inserted in the center of the meat reads 140°F (60°C), about 1 hour. Transfer veal to a cutting board to rest.

Put the vinegar and bread in a bowl. Let bread soak, then squeeze it dry and discard vinegar.

Deglaze the roasting pan with white wine. Simmer until the wine evaporates, then add the capers, anchovies, tuna and bread. Cook for a few minutes.

Transfer the mixture to a blender. Add the hard-cooked egg yolks and blend, gradually adding veal or beef stock until sauce is smooth and creamy. Thinly slice the veal and serve with the sauce.

# VOL-AU-VENT
## WITH RADICCHIO AND FONDUE

*Preparation time: 10 minutes   Cooking time: 15 minutes   Difficulty: easy*

**4 SERVINGS**

12 **vol-au-vents** (puff-pastry shells)
6 oz. (170 g) **Fontina cheese**, coarsely chopped
1 1/4 cups (300 ml) **lukewarm milk**
2 large **egg yolks**
2 tsp. (5 g) **all-purpose flour**
**Black truffle** (optional)
10 1/2 oz. (300 g) **red radicchio**, coarsely chopped
**Salt** to taste

Whisk the egg yolks with 2 tablespoons of milk and set aside.
In another bowl, whisk the flour into the remaining milk, then add the Fontina.
Transfer the mixture to a saucepan and cook over medium heat, whisking vigorously, until the mixture thickens.
Add the egg yolk mixture, reduce heat to low, and continue to cook, whisking occasionally, for about 10 minutes.
Keep the mixture warm. Season with salt and stir in the radicchio. Evenly distribute the mixture to the vol-au-vents and serve, garnished with freshly grated black truffle, if desired.

# INGREDIENTS INDEX

# PHOTO CREDITS

All photographs are by ACADEMIA BARILLA except the following:
pages 6, 95 ©123RF

WHITE STAR PUBLISHERS

WS White Star Publishers® is a registered trademark
property of De Agostini Libri S.p.A.

© 2013 De Agostini Libri S.p.A.
Via G. da Verrazano, 15 - 28100 Novara, Italy
www.whitestar.it - www.deagostini.it

Translations:
Catherine Howard - Mary Doyle - John Venerella - Free z'be, Paris
Salvatore Ciolfi - Rosetta Translations SARL - Rosetta Translations SARL

ISBN 978-88-544-0739-8
1 2 3 4 5 6    16 15 14 13 12

Printed in China